Get Inside Baseball

by Paul Almonte

illustrations by Donna Salvini

SILVER MOON PRESS
NEW YORK

First Silver Moon Press Edition 1994

Copyright © 1994 by Paul Almonte
Illustration copyright © 1994 by Donna Salvini

For information contact:
Silver Moon Press
126 Fifth Avenue
Suite 803
New York, NY 10011
(800) 874-3320

Designed by Donna Salvini
Illustrated by Donna Salvini

Photograph Credits: cover, permission for
use granted by Bettmann Archives; p. 13, Copyright by Robert Payne.
Photo by Earl Davis Payne, electrical engineer who, along with others,
designed the lights at Crosley Field; all other photos courtesy
of the National Baseball Hall of Fame and Museum, Inc.

Library of Congress Cataloging-in-Publication Information:

Almonte, Paul.
Get Inside Baseball / by Paul Almonte
p. cm.
"Get Inside."
ISBN 1-881889-55-6 : $12.95
ISBN (Paperback edition) 1-881889-58-0 : $6.95
1. Baseball—United States—History—Juvenile literature.
[1. Baseball—History.] I. Title.
GV867.5.A46 1994
796.357'0973—dc20
93-41625

10 9 8 7 6 5 4 3 2 1

Printed in the USA

Table of Contents

INTRODUCTION

Whether played by boys and girls in sandlots or parks, or by professionals before 50,000 fans at Yankee Stadium, baseball is about America. It is about one way we share dreams of being winners, of setting goals and reaching them. Baseball is about how and why many of us grow up wanting to be like Willie Mays or Joe DiMaggio, Nolan Ryan, Roberto Clemente, or Barry Bonds. Baseball is also about an important part of American history. From teaching us to overcome prejudice to giving us role models for sportsmanship and hard work, baseball is truly America's game. This book will give you a look at baseball—its past and its present—and a look at the players and people who make this game so much fun, so exciting, and so important for so many fans.

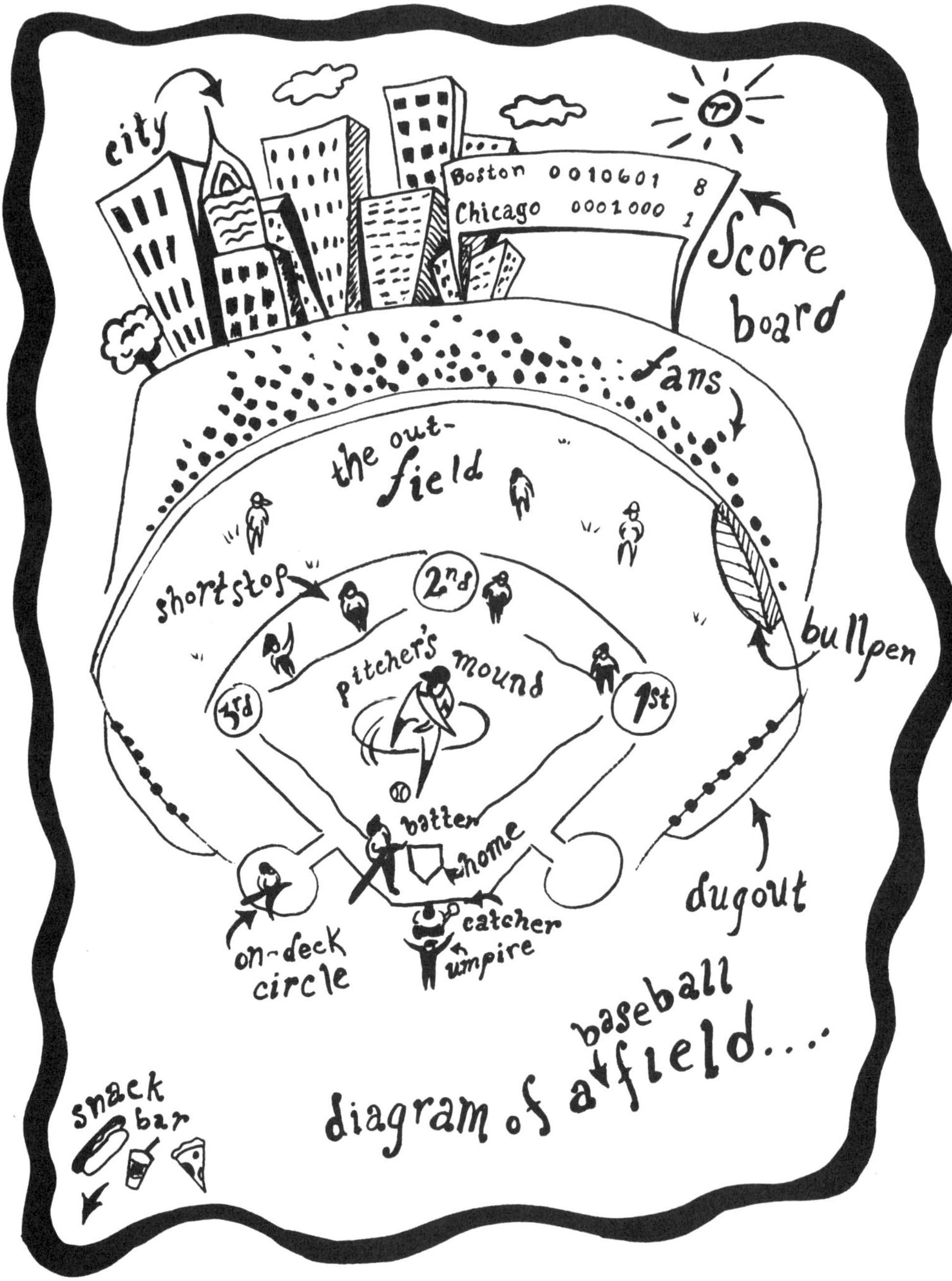

city

| Boston | 0010601 | 8 |
| Chicago | 0001000 | 1 |

Score board

fans

the out-field

shortstop

2nd

pitcher's mound

3rd

1st

bullpen

batter

home

dugout

on-deck circle

catcher

umpire

snack bar

diagram of a baseball field....

1

How the Game Got Started

Although some people may believe that a man named
Abner Doubleday invented baseball in 1839, games that
resemble what would become baseball were played in the
United States for many years before 1839. In fact, baseball
may have come from England. The British had a game called
"rounders," in which the main idea was to hit a ball thrown by
a "feeder" (pitcher) and run bases. Rounders was known and
played in America long before Abner Doubleday supposedly
invented baseball as we now know it. A "Base Ball" poem,
written in 1744 in England, supports the idea that the English
were playing games similar to modern baseball as early as
the 18th century:

The ball once struck off,
Away flies the boy
To the next destined point,
And then home with joy.

Historians now recognize a man named Alexander Cartwright as the actual inventor of modern baseball. Cartwright wrote the rules of a sport that closely resembled today's game. He was the person who decided that each team would use nine players at a time. He also originated the "three outs per inning" rule and the idea that a team could not change its batting order. Cartwright set the bases—which were then stakes—30 paces apart. One big difference in the game Cartwright played, however, was that runners were out when the defense hit them with a thrown ball! Another difference from today's game was that a team won when it reached 21 runs. It wasn't until 1857 that the nine-inning format came into use. The first match using Cartwright's rules was played at the Elysian Fields in Hoboken, New Jersey, on June 19, 1846. To explain his rules to all the players, Cartwright "umpired" that first game.

The first professional baseball team was organized in 1869 by a man named Harry Wright. He rounded up nine other men to play with him and named his team the Cincinnati Red Stockings. The Red Stockings played amateur teams around the country and didn't lose a game all year. In fact, they won 99 consecutive games before they finally lost one in 1870. Perhaps their greatest victory was a win over a team called the Buckeyes. The Stockings beat them 103 to 8!

The Red Stockings were very popular. Fan interest led to the organization of a professional league. It was called the National Association of Professional Base Ball Players. But from its beginnings in 1871, dishonesty and gambling plagued the league. The National Association quickly went out of business.

A year after this failed attempt, another league was formed. It was called the National League. The league established rules to govern players' and owners' conduct. Eight professional teams flourished under the National League. In 1882, a rival league was formed. It was called the American Association. When competition for the best players heated up, the leagues agreed to reserve the right to keep certain players. In 1884, the two leagues agreed to the first post-season playoff competition. The winners of each league would compete in a series to determine a "world" champion.

In 1900, the American League was reformed from what was left of the minor Western League. This eight-team league—which had clubs in Baltimore, Buffalo, Chicago, Cleveland, Detroit, Milwaukee, Philadelphia, and Washington, DC—also competed for National League players. Some stars, including Napoleon Lajoie, who was later to be elected to the Hall of Fame, jumped to this new league.

By 1903, the two leagues were ready to stop fighting for players. Together they formed a major league baseball organization. Teams played within their own leagues, and the champions of each league met in a "World's Series" competition. The leagues agreed to respect the contracts players signed with individual teams. This was the beginning of Major League Baseball as we know it today.

Modern baseball developed in part through the players who have become known for their on-field heroics and off-the-field exploits. Here are a few of the greatest ones:

BABE RUTH

Baseball became more and more popular during the 20th century, but one player stands out as the person who made baseball the national pastime of the United States. His name was Babe Ruth. Prior to Ruth's emergence as a home-run hitter and major crowd attraction, baseball did not have a superstar. When Ruth joined the Yankees (his contract had been sold to them by the Boston Red Sox), he led a team that dominated Major League

Baseball for decades. In 1927, Ruth hit an incredible 60 home runs in a single season, a record that stood for 34 years until Roger Maris hit 61 homers in 1961. With fans pouring in by the thousands to see "The Babe," Yankee Stadium became known as "The House that Ruth Built."

Ruth's legend goes far beyond outstanding statistics. He was a larger-than-life figure, who some say could even "call his shots," hitting home runs when he wanted to. It is said that in a World Series game against the Chicago Cubs in 1932, Ruth actually pointed to the spot where he was going to hit a homer and then hammered the ball to that exact spot.

LOU GEHRIG

In the 1920s, the New York Yankees were the undisputed kings of baseball. The flamboyant Babe Ruth, the "Sultan of Swat," hit monster home runs and drew huge crowds. But the Yankees also had another superstar, first baseman Lou Gehrig. Gehrig was a New York boy; he had played college ball for Columbia University. When he signed with the Yankees, Gehrig teamed with Ruth to lead them to many World Series wins.

Gehrig's career stats—including 493 home runs, a .340 batting average, and a major league record 23 career grand slam home runs—landed him in the Hall of Fame. Among his many records, Gehrig played in an amazing 2,130 consecutive games. This durability earned him the nickname "The Iron Horse." Unfortunately, Gehrig's playing streak and career ended tragically. During the beginning of the 1939 season, Gehrig was not playing well. He often felt weak and dizzy. Fans and players alike thought he was finished, an over-the-hill player past his prime.

After a particularly bad game, Gehrig took himself out of the lineup. He went to a doctor to find out what was wrong. It turned out he had a rare disease, Amyotrophic Lateral Sclerosis (ALS). This disease attacks the body's muscle and nerve centers. There is no cure. Gehrig never played another game.

Gehrig retired from baseball, but he continued to work hard. He taught people about his illness and raised money for research for a cure. To this day, ALS is known as "Lou Gehrig's Disease." Two years before his death, the Yankees held a special "Lou Gehrig's Day" at Yankee Stadium. Thousands of fans, including Babe Ruth, gave Lou a standing ovation. Gehrig wanted people to know that he was not bitter about what had happened to him. In the most moving line of his speech, Gehrig thanked the crowd for their support, saying he considered himself "the luckiest man on the face of the earth."

JACKIE ROBINSON

In 1945, a man named Branch Rickey did something that would change the course of baseball history. Rickey was the owner of the Brooklyn Dodgers and also a man who cared deeply about the game of baseball. For a long time, Rickey had felt that Major League Baseball should be open to all the best players, regardless of race. He felt that baseball should not be segregated and he knew that many minority athletes were as good as the game's white players. The members of the Negro Leagues played great baseball. Stars like Josh Gibson and Satchel Paige could just have easily have been stars in the Major Leagues, as well.

Rickey was looking for a black player with special qualities. Not only did this player have to be talented, but he also had to be able to handle the pressure of being the first black ballplayer in the majors. Rickey knew it would be tough. Segregation was practiced in many parts of the country. Many white people still felt that blacks were inferior and shouldn't be allowed in the front of the bus, let alone in the modern Major Leagues. Rickey knew that the player he chose to "break the color barrier" was going to be called "nigger" and possibly even physically attacked for joining the Major Leagues.

Rickey finally made his choice: Jackie Robinson. Robinson was a superb athlete who had been playing for the Kansas City Monarchs of the Negro Leagues. Rickey invited Robinson to visit him in New York. There he told Robinson of his plan to have him become the first black player in Major League Baseball. Robinson agreed. He was sent to the Montreal Royals, the Dodgers' minor league club, for the 1946 season.

Robinson showed that Branch Rickey had been right to select him. Robinson hit a home run in his first game with the Royals. He led the International League in batting and helped his team to the league title.

At the beginning of the 1947 season, Branch Rickey felt it was time to introduce Robinson to the Major Leagues. Unfortunately, Robinson's debut in the big leagues was not as good as his start in the minors. He was nervous and didn't get a hit in his first few games. In addition, fans were yelling insults. Even opposing players—and some teammates—were treating him with prejudice. Through it all, Robinson kept his dignity. He soon overcame his nervousness and started playing terrific baseball. As the Dodgers' second baseman, he batted .297 for his first year, led the Dodgers in home runs, and led the league in stolen bases. He was voted the National League Rookie of the Year (an award given to the best new player in the league).

In later years, Jackie became an even greater star. He was the National League's Most Valuable Player in 1949, and helped the Dodgers make it to six World Series.

As other players, owners, and fans saw that Robinson was a terrific player they overcame their prejudice. There were still a few incidents, but most people came to accept the desegregation of baseball. In 1948 and 1949, many other major league teams rushed to sign other black players, as well as Latino stars, especially Cubans. In a few short years, Jackie Robinson and Branch Rickey had broken the color barrier and made baseball "America's Game" for Americans of every color and race.

NOLAN RYAN

Hard-throwing fireballer Nolan Ryan is a hero to many fans. They love him for many reasons: because he's the greatest strikeout pitcher of all time (by the end of the 1993 season, Ryan had struck out a record 5,714 batters); because of his record seven no-hitters; and also because he played a young man's game for an incredible 27 seasons. Ryan, who retired from baseball after the 1993 season, was pitching and winning at the age of 46.

Ryan began his career with the New York Mets in 1966. Though he did not become a star overnight (he didn't even have a winning record for a number of years), he did have one thing. Ryan threw one of the fastest fastballs in baseball. Year in and year out, Ryan was among the leaders in strikeouts. As he began to master his curveball and control his fastball, Ryan became a true superstar. In addition to his no-hitters, Ryan has been on a winning World Series team (the Miracle Mets of 1969), won 324 major league ballgames, and struck out 19 batters in a single game four times. In five years, when he becomes eligible for admission, we are sure to see Ryan in the Hall of Fame.

Nolan Ryan, after his third no-hitter

NIGHT BASEBALL

Night baseball? The critics laughed. "Night baseball will never become popular with the fans," they said. But Cincinnati Reds general manager Larry MacPhail knew better. So he had lights installed at Crosley Field, where the Reds played. On May 24, 1935, the first major league game "under the lights" was played. Over 20,000 fans saw the Reds beat the Philadelphia Phillies 2 to 1.

The 1947 Muskegon Lassies, of the Women's League

A Japanese Athletic baseball team

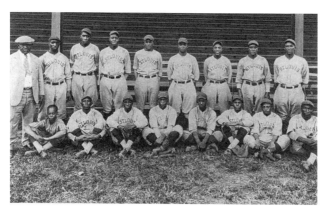

The 1928 St. Louis Stars, of the Negro Leagues

CHAPTER 2
All Kinds of Leagues

Today, all major league teams own or are affiliated with a series of minor league teams. These teams, called "farm" teams, are used to train and instruct young players, and to get them ready for the majors. The minor leagues are organized by player levels or classes. Triple A teams include those players closest to making it to the majors. They are followed by Double A, Single A, and Rookie League teams.

In the early years of baseball, minor league clubs were not so closely associated with major league teams. The minor leagues were made up of teams from cities, usually small ones, that didn't have major league teams. Today, minor and major league affiliations are closer relationships. Major league clubs often provide financial support for their minor league counterparts.

Life in the minor leagues is very different from life in the big leagues. Instead of million-dollar contracts and chartered plane rides between cities, the minors offer smaller paychecks and long bus rides from one small town to another. Instead of playing ball in front of more than 50,000 fans, minor leaguers can expect to play in front of "crowds" of hundreds.

LITTLE LEAGUE

Organized baseball starts long before the minor leagues. Many boys and girls play some type of organized baseball while growing up. The idea for a kids' "little" league was actually thought up by a man named Carl E. Stotz of Williamsport, Pennsylvania. In 1939, he put together three teams made up of boys aged eight to twelve. Soon, the idea caught on. By 1947, a league was begun in nearby New Jersey. That year also saw the first Little League World Series. It was played in Williamsport, Pennsylvania, and was won by the Maynard team from Williamsport. The idea of a kids' World Series spurred interest in Little Leagues all over America. By 1954, 3,000 leagues were in operation in the United States. Soon leagues were formed in Canada. Countries in Europe and Asia quickly developed their own Little League teams.

Today, the Little League World Series truly is a world event, though it is still played in Williamsport each year. Teams from 75 countries participate in tournaments that lead up to the World Series. In fact, in recent years, teams from outside the United States have won most of the series: Out of the past 20 series, teams from Taiwan have won *11* championships.

Unfortunately, with the intense interest in the Little League World Series has come an intense pressure on teams and countries to win. Some teams have cheated by using players who were too old to play. In fact, the 1992 winner, a team from Zamboanga City in the Philippines, was stripped of its title after it was discovered that the team had used eight overage players. Their opponent in the finals, a team from Long Beach, California, was crowned the World Series champ instead.

The 1993 preliminary tournaments saw two more teams—one from China and one from the Dominican Republic—disqualified for using ineligible players. But these actions didn't detract from one of the most exciting Series games in Little League history. The Long Beach, California, team again reached the final game. They played a team from David, Panama. The close game was tied 2-2 as the teams entered the sixth, and final, inning. Panama couldn't score in their half of the inning. In the bottom of the inning, Long

Beach loaded the bases. A twelve-year old named Jeremy Hess came up as a pinch hitter. He hit a shot off the wall 204 feet away to knock in the series-winning run. The Long Beach team had done what no other U.S. Little League team had ever done—they'd won two Series in a row!

1993 saw another important Little League World Series first. Kathy Bernard, a third base coach for a team from Canada, became the first woman to coach in the tournament. Though her team didn't reach the finals, Bernard showed the world that baseball is a game for girls and women as well as for boys and men.

THE NEGRO LEAGUES

Before Branch Rickey signed Jackie Robinson to become the first player to break the color line, black baseball players played in their own leagues. These were called the Negro Leagues. Teams of black players traveled the country, playing before huge crowds. In addition to Jackie Robinson, many future stars in the majors first played in the Negro Leagues. Roy Campanella, Willie Mays, and Ernie Banks all got their starts in these leagues. Though excluded from the majors until 1947, Negro Leagues players did often play against major league stars during off-season tours and exhibitions. And they often won.

Unfortunately, a number of top black players didn't get a chance to show their best stuff against the white major leaguers because they were too old when the majors finally integrated. Two of the best examples are Satchel Paige and Josh Gibson. Though Paige did play a few years in the majors, his best playing was done in the Negro Leagues. Over his career, Paige pitched in over 2500 games and threw an amazing 45 no-hitters. Baseball fans found out just how good Paige was when he pitched exhibition games against teams of major league stars. In one such game, played in 1934, Paige pitched against All-Star Dizzy Dean. While Dean allowed only one run in 13 innings, Paige did him one better. He struck out 17 men and didn't give up a single run.

Paige's greatest accomplishment might have been his longevity. He pitched his first Negro Leagues game in 1926. In 1965, 39 years later, Paige ended his career pitching in the majors.

Josh Gibson was perhaps the best player never to play in the majors. A catcher, Gibson was known as the "black Babe Ruth." Gibson hit 75 homers in one season (1931). Gibson also had an astounding .457 batting average in 1936. Roy Campanella, who was to become a major league star with the Dodgers, was a catcher in the Negro Leagues when Gibson was in his prime. Of Gibson's talent Campanella said, "I couldn't carry Josh's glove. Anything I could do, he could do better." Unfortunately, Gibson never got his chance in the majors. He died three months before Robinson's color-line breakthrough.

In addition to the recognition the Negro Leagues have received from the Baseball Hall of Fame, a new museum will document the history of these leagues. In a few years, a museum devoted to black history will open in Kansas City. Included will be an exhibit called "Discover Greatness! An Illustrated History of Negro Leagues Baseball." The exhibit features memorabilia and information about the leagues and their players. It is currently traveling the country (its first stop was at the 1993 Major League All-Star Game). Then it will go on permanent display in the museum in Kansas City.

The history of the Negro Leagues also includes a little-known but important baseball fact. It was in these leagues that the only woman to have regularly played in a men's professional league competed. Toni Stone, from St. Paul, Minnesota, played for the New Orleans Creoles in 1949, the Indianapolis Clowns from 1951 to '53, and the Kansas City Monarchs in 1954.

THE WOMEN'S LEAGUE

In 1992, a movie called *A League of Their Own* brought attention to another important part of baseball history. The

movie was about a women's professional baseball league and
was based on the women's league that operated in the United
States from 1943 to 1954. Called the "All-American Girls'
Professional Baseball League," the league was the idea
of Philip Wrigley, then owner of the Chicago Cubs. In 1942,
Wrigley was worried that World War II was going to
force the Major Leagues to cancel their season because many
players were being drafted into the army. His idea was to create
a women's league for fans to watch instead. Though the
majors were not completely shut down, the women's league
eventually became very popular.

The league was made up of teams from the Midwest.
They had names like the Rockford Peaches and the Springfield
Sallies. The league schedule was tough. Teams played up to
127 games in a season and often played every day of the week.
The All-American Girls' League played top-notch baseball and
has records that male major leaguers may never match. One
player, Sophie Kurys of the Racine Belles, stole more bases in
her career than even Rickey Henderson has. In ten seasons,
Kurys stole 1,114 bases. In one year, Kurys stole an incredible
201 bases in 203 attempts. And while people make much of
the fact that stars like Barry Bonds and Ken Griffey, Jr. got
their baseball skills from their major league dads (Bobby
Bonds and Ken Griffey, Sr., respectively), a recent major lea-
guer can thank his baseball-playing mom. Casey Candaele of

the Houston Astros is the son of former Fort Wayne Daisy player Helen Callaghan St. Aubin.

Though the league's popularity slowly dwindled as the war ended and the Major Leagues got back to full strength, the All-American Girls' League did draw a lot of fans during its twelve-year existence. The league's history is documented by a permanent display—called "Women in Baseball"—in the Baseball Hall of Fame.

1994 saw two firsts for women in baseball. The first all-female minor-league baseball team, the Colorado Silver Bullets, began playing exhibition games this year. The team is recognized by the National Association of Professional Baseball Leagues, and is managed by former major league pitcher Phil Niekro. And Ila Borders, a student at Southern California College, became the first woman to pitch in a college baseball game. In her first start, Borders, a left-hander, pitched a complete game and struck out two batters. Southern California College beat the Claremont Mudd-Scripps, 12-1.

THE JAPANESE LEAGUE

Baseball is not only America's game. It is Japan's national pastime, too. People in Japan were learning the game as early as 1869. That year, an American missionary in Japan named Horace Wilson taught baseball to his students.

In the 1920s and 1930s, American major leaguers visited Japan
to play exhibitions. Players like Babe Ruth became as popular
there as in the States.

In 1936, Japan's first professional league began playing.
Through the years, the Japanese Leagues' popularity has
grown. One reason for their success was the huge popularity of
their most famous player: Sadaharu Oh. Oh played for the
Yomiuri Giants. Oh slugged 868 home runs in his 22-year
career, more than either Babe Ruth or Hank Aaron. (Aaron, a
star player for the Milwaukee and Atlanta Braves, broke Ruth's
home-run record, finishing his career with a total of 755 round-
trippers.) Besides surpassing Aaron's career record, Oh also
won 15 home run titles and was his league's Most Valuable
Player nine times.

A number of American players have gone to Japan to play
ball. In many cases, the Americans were the best players on
their Japanese teams. Many of them were at the end of their
careers in the States and were lured by high salaries. One
exception to this rule was Cecil Fielder. Fielder was unhappy as
a part-time player for the Toronto Blue Jays, so he accepted an
offer to play in Japan for the Hanshin Tigers. After a strong season in which he hit 38 homers and batted .302, Fielder
returned to the American majors and has become a star
slugger with the Detroit Tigers. In his first year with the Tigers,
Fielder hit 51 home runs.

C H A P T E R
3

The Baseball Season

THE FRONT OFFICE

Besides the players, many more people are involved in preparing a team for a game or a season. Members of the "front office," the people who run the team, include a general manager, a public relations officer, and scouts. General managers are the ones who usually trade players to other teams or decide which free agents (players who are no longer under contract to a particular team) to sign to contracts. They also hire—and fire—managers.

Scouts will watch other teams play and offer reports about what teams are doing, which players are playing well, or what the hitting looks like.

Team managers often help decide which players should be on the team. They will work with the general manager to decide what the team needs (a new relief pitcher, for example, or a back-up shortstop). Managers also decide game strategy. They begin by filling out a starting line-up card that shows who is playing what position and when they are batting. Managers also decide when to use pinch hitters and relief pitchers.

The manager has a number of other people working for him. He has coaches who are responsible for particular aspects of a team. For example, he will have a pitching coach who helps the pitchers develop new pitching motions, strategies, or even new pitches. A batting coach, or hitting instructor, will give advice to the hitters on his team.

Coaches are also used during the game. The first base and third base coaches position themselves near these two bases while their team is batting. They are responsible for signaling to batters and runners what the manager wants them to do in a particular situation. For example, a third base coach might signal to a batter not to swing at a pitch because the runner on first is going to try to steal second base. The coach does this by "flashing" a pre-determined signal (maybe touching his cap, or his belt buckle) to the batter. Meanwhile, the runner on first has received a similar signal, or maybe a verbal one, from the first base coach. This signaling method allows the players to work together.

ON THE FIELD

From the team mascot to the umpires, from the bat boy or bat girl to the hot dog vendors, there are many other people involved in making a day at the ballpark fun.

Fans want to know about their favorite players and teams. Sportswriters from local and national newspapers and magazines cover the team, often traveling with the players from city to city to provide information to the readers and viewers.

Safe!

Out!

Catcher flashing signs to his pitcher

Base coach sending signs to a batter or base runner

Writers and TV and radio announcers interview players before and after games.

Other than the players and managers, there are no people more important to a baseball game than the four umpires (fewer in the Minor Leagues). These people make the calls—ball or strike, safe or out—that can decide the outcome of a ballgame. The umpires must know all the rules and apply them fairly to both teams. Major league umpires are very experienced. They go to umpiring schools and work for years in the minors before umpiring a game at the major league level.

SPRING TRAINING

Before the baseball season begins, teams go to their training camps in the southern or western part of the United States where it is warm enough to play outdoors in March. There they get in shape for the coming season. Spring training, as this practice time is called, is a time for young players to try to make the big club and for veterans to work on their batting eyes. Some players use spring training to work on a new position. All players work on the the basic plays they need to know, and basic skills like bunting, "turning a double-play," and fielding their positions. Managers will invite many players to training camp and then choose the best players "to take north" to start the regular season. They look at how well the players do in a series of exhibition games—practice games that do not count in the regular season league standings against other ball clubs. By the time the season starts, the managers have decided on their 25-man roster. Teams usually carry 10 or 11 pitchers and 2 or 3 catchers. The rest of the team is comprised of outfielders and infielders. Some players will be reserves, who can fill in for everyday players in case they are sick, injured, or just tired. Often, these reserve, or utility, players are able to play a number of different positions.

Today, there are two spring training sites in the United States, Florida and Arizona. The teams are organized into two unofficial leagues. The Florida league is called the Grapefruit League; the Arizona league is known as the Cactus League.

Spring training has been a part of baseball from the beginning of the professional leagues. In 1884, the Boston team from the National League spent time in New Orleans preparing for the upcoming season. The very next year, two more teams—Pittsburgh and Louisville—went south for some pre-season practice. In 1886, the Chicago White Stockings team went to Hot Springs, Arkansas, for a series of pre-season workouts because their manager, Cap Anson, thought the team was out of shape. Today, keeping in condition is a year-round job for all ball players. But spring training still serves its main purpose: to get the whole team ready to play together for the full season ahead of them.

OPENING DAY

For many fans, the first day of the baseball season is the best day of the year. Perhaps Opening Day holds this special appeal because only on this day is every team equal. Players and fans alike can all hope that their team is going to go on to win the World Series.

Opening Day has always been marked by special activities. One special tradition has been having the President of the United States "throw out the first ball" to signal the beginning of the new season. President William Taft began this tradition.

A DAY AT THE GAME

Before the umpire yells "Play Ball" to start a game, players and team staff alike have a lot to do. Players usually arrive at the ballpark hours in advance. All players will stretch or do calisthenics to prepare for the coming game. Pitchers and catchers will go over how they want to pitch certain hitters on the opposing team. Players will take batting and fielding practice to stay sharp. Coaches will meet to decide strategy, such as who should play which position.

THE ALL-STAR GAME

In 1933, a reporter named Arch Ward, who worked for a newspaper in Chicago, came up with an idea to promote the

World's Fair being held in Chicago that year. He thought it would be exciting for the best players from the National and American Leagues to play a game against each other. Ward's idea became known as the All-Star Game.

Played at mid-season in a different major league ballpark each year, the All-Star Game has become a great spectacle. Fans select their favorite players to start the game. They fill out ballots given to them at ballgames during the first half of the season. After the fans select the starters, the two managers select reserve players and pitchers. To make sure every fan has a hometown player to root for, at least one player from each team must be chosen for the game. Of course, the best teams often have as many as six or seven players chosen.

Some of the greatest moments in baseball history have occurred in All-Star Games. In 1934, a National League pitcher named Carl Hubbell put on an amazing pitching exhibition. Facing a powerful American League lineup, Hubbell struck out five All-Stars in a row, including Babe Ruth and Lou Gehrig.

Home-run hitters have often been the stars of the All-Star Game. In fact, Babe Ruth helped the American League win the first All-Star game in 1933 by hitting a two-run homer. Super-stars like Ted Williams, Stan Musial, and Hank Aaron have all hit round-trippers to win All-Star Games. More recently, young stars like Bo Jackson and Ken Griffey, Jr. have put on power displays in the mid-season classic. With sluggers like these leading the way, the American League has been able to win the last six All-Star Games.

PENNANT RACES AND PLAYOFFS

Before 1969, the top team from each league went straight to the World Series. The ends of each season were often very exciting as teams battled to win their league title or pennant. Often these pennant races, or "stretch runs" as they are called, make for tense, close races. One of the most famous pennant races was in 1951. That year, the Brooklyn Dodgers and the New York Giants finished the regular season tied. They had to

Left: Bo Jackson in his Kansas City Royals uniform Right: Bo stepping into his swing

play three games to decide which team would play against the New York Yankees in the World Series.

During the regular season, no one expected there would be any need for a playoff. In mid-August, the Dodgers led the Giants by as many as $13\frac{1}{2}$ games. But the Giants came back. They compiled an incredible record of 37 wins and only 7 losses in August and September. At the end of the year the teams were tied. Each team won one of the first two games of the playoff. In the third and deciding game, Dodger pitching ace Don Newcombe took a 4-1 lead into the bottom of the ninth inning. With two men on and one out, the Giants' Whitey Lockman hit a run-scoring double. The score was now 4-2 Dodgers, with Giant runners on second and third. At this point, Ralph Branca replaced Newcombe as pitcher. The Giants' batter was Bobby Thomson.

Thomson had hit a homer off Branca in the first playoff game. After taking one pitch, Thomson stepped back into the batter's box to face Branca's second pitch. It was an inside fastball. Thomson swung and smashed the ball over the left-field fence for a three-run homer! The hit became known as the "Shot Heard 'Round the World," and it gave the Giants a victory over the Dodgers and sent the team into the World Series against the New York Yankees.

In 1969, both the American and National Leagues split their teams into two separate divisions. This realignment changed how the playoffs would operate. The teams with the best records in each division faced each other in a League Championship Series. The winner of each playoff series then competed against the other League's champion in the World Series.

Beginning in 1994, the old two-divisions-in-a-league format gave way to a new arrangement. Three divisions were established in both the American and the National Leagues (some teams were moved out of their old divisions). Under the reorganization, four teams in each league got to go to the playoffs: the three division-winners plus one "wild card" team, to make things more exciting.

This reorganization has made the race to the Series more complicated than it used to be, but it also promises the possibility for thrilling games. And since the wild card teams have been included, the chance that a team will pull off a "Cinderella" season has been increased, coming from behind in the last days to win it all.

Of course, not everyone agrees that the new format is such a great idea. In baseball, there is no shortage of opinions on how the game should be played. The playoffs have certainly been terrifically exciting in the past, even when the team that might have deserved to win failed to capture a victory in the end.

In 1978 and 1992, two of the most exciting races to the World Series took place.

1978: BUCKY DENT BREAKS HEARTS IN BEANTOWN

In the middle of the 1978 season, the Boston Red Sox looked to be a good bet to win the American League East pennant and go on to face the American League West winner in the Championship Series. They were well ahead of their nearest rivals. Even the powerful New York Yankees weren't offering much of a challenge. Red Sox fans were looking forward to their first World Series championship since 1918. But something happened—the Sox began to fade, and the Yankees charged ahead. By the end of the 162-game regular schedule, the two teams were tied. A one-game playoff, in Boston, was played to decide which team would face the Kansas City Royals for the league championship.

As the game entered the middle innings, it looked as if Boston would win. The Red Sox led 2-0, and their pitcher, Mike Torrez, was keeping the Yankees bats quiet. Then the Yankees got two men on base and shortstop Bucky Dent stepped to the plate. Torrez delivered a pitch, and Dent, to the amazement of everyone in the stands—players and fans alike—hit the pitch over the left-field fence for a three-run homer. The Red Sox never recovered. They lost 5-4 and the Yankees went on to beat the Royals for the American League Championship. The

Yankees completed their spectacular season by beating the Dodgers to win their second consecutive World Series title.

1992: BRAVES VS. PIRATES

The National League Championship Series between the Pittsburgh Pirates and the Atlanta Braves was one of the most dramatic ever played. First of all, it was a rematch. The Pirates and Braves had met the year before, and the Braves had won the 1991 Series, 4 games to 3. Now the Pirates were looking for revenge.

Just like in 1991, the 1992 Series went to seven games. In the final and deciding contest, pitching ace Doug Drabek started for Pittsburgh. John Smoltz was on the pitcher's mound for the Braves. Pittsburgh, with runs in the first and sixth innings, took their two-run lead into the bottom of the ninth. Atlanta had only one more chance to win the game.

In the ninth inning, the Braves got to Drabek. Terry Pendleton, the Braves' third baseman, hit a double. Then, Dave Justice got on base on an error, and Sid Bream walked. The bases were loaded. Pirate manager Jim Leyland replaced Drabek with relief pitcher Stan Belinda. Belinda gave up a sacrifice fly to Ron Gant. The next batter, Damon Berryhill, walked. The bases were again loaded. Brian Hunter hit a pop fly which Jose Lind caught. There were now two outs and the Pirates still led 2 to 1. Braves manager Bobby Cox sent up a pinch hitter, Francisco Cabrera. Down to their last out, the Braves and their 51,000 fans needed a miracle. And they got one. Cabrera hit a single which knocked in two runs to beat the Pirates and send the Braves into the World Series.

CHAPTER 4
The World Series

The World Series. The name says it all. The best teams from the National and American Leagues play a best-four-of-seven series to decide which team will rule the baseball world. The games are seen by tens of millions of fans around the world. Players become stars—or bums—with their performance in the Series. Reggie Jackson became a superstar, "Mr. October," by helping the Oakland A's and the New York Yankees win World Series titles. Bob Gibson won two World Series Most Valuable Player awards by pitching the St. Louis Cardinals to wins in 1964 and 1967. Players and fans alike anticipate the drama and tension that the World Series always seems to bring.

1903: THE FIRST WORLD SERIES

Post-season championship series had been played between rival baseball leagues as early as 1883. But it was not until 1903 that the Major Leagues decided to have a series between National and American League winners to decide a world champion. This World Series was not considered such a big deal. But it did serve its purpose—to crown a "world" champion. That year, the Boston club of the American League beat the Pittsburgh club of the National League, 5 games to 3, in a best-of-nine series.

Here is a look at some of the key World Series match-ups of this century:

1919: THE "BLACK SOX" SCANDAL

The Chicago White Sox, with their star "Shoeless" Joe Jackson to lead them, were heavily favored to beat the Cincinnati Reds in the 1919 World Series. Surprisingly, the White Sox didn't win. The Reds beat the White Sox 5 games to 3 and fans across the country just couldn't believe it. Soon they found out why. Joe Jackson and a number of his teammates had allegedly agreed to "throw the Series"—they purposely lost games so the other team would win. They made errors in the field and hit and pitched poorly during key moments in a number of the games. In return, Jackson and his teammates were to receive money from gamblers who planned to bet a lot of money on the Reds.

When this scandal was discovered, fans were outraged. They were afraid to trust the players. The "Black" Sox, as they were soon called, had given baseball a black eye. Baseball officials knew something had to be done, so they hired a commissioner, Kenesaw Mountain Landis, who had been a Federal judge. It was his job to see that the rules of the game were obeyed. Landis banned Jackson and the other "Black" Sox from ever playing major league baseball again. He helped restore the fans' faith in the integrity of the game.

1927: THE "MURDERERS' ROW" YANKEES

The 1927 World Series pitted the Pittsburgh Pirates of the National League against the American League New York Yankees. Few fans gave Pittsburgh any chance of beating the Yankees. After all, the Yankees were led by two of the greatest players of all time: Lou Gehrig and Babe Ruth. Ruth had hit 60 home runs during the regular season, and Gehrig had chipped in with a whopping 175 runs batted in. The Yankees also had two other players, Bob Meusel and Tony Lazzeri, who had over 100 RBIs each. Such slugging power gave the team their nickname—the "Murderers' Row." The Yankees' hitters murdered just about every ball pitched to them. To no one's surprise, the

Yankees didn't disappoint their fans in the 1927 World Series. They beat the Pirates in 4 straight games.

1960: THE PITTSBURGH PIRATES VERSUS THE NEW YORK YANKEES

If you look at the stats for the first six games of the 1960 Series, you might think that the Yankees had walloped the Pirates (who had been outscored 46-17 to that point). But that wasn't the case. The Series was tied at 3 games each, and game seven was to be played at Pittsburgh's home field. The last game was a seesaw affair, with the lead going back and forth between the two teams. The Pirates struck first, scoring four runs in the first two innings. The Yankees then battled back to take a 5-4 lead. They added two more runs and had a 7-4 advantage going into the bottom of the eighth inning. But then it was the Pirates' turn to fight back. They scored five runs and went back in front 9-7.

In the top of the ninth, it looked as if the Pirates would be champs. They only needed to record three more Yankee outs. But the Yankees would not go down without one last fight. They scored two runs to tie the score at nine. The game was truly in its last, most dramatic moments. The Pirates had a chance to win. Yankee pitcher Ralph Terry was set to pitch to the first batter, Pirate second baseman Bill Mazeroski. The first pitch was a ball. On Terry's second delivery, Mazeroski swung and sent the ball over the left field fence for a home run. This was the first home run ever to win a World Series in the last inning of the last game!

1969: THE AMAZIN' METS

The New York Mets had made a terrific stretch run to catch the Cubs and win the National League East pennant. And they defeated the Atlanta Braves in the National League Championship. Despite this, the Mets were still underdogs to beat the powerful Baltimore Orioles in the 1969 World Series. After all, the Orioles had home-run sluggers Boog Powell and Frank Robinson and top pitchers including Mike Cuellar and Jim Palmer. And the Mets? Well, before this season, the Mets had never finished higher than *ninth* place in their league.

When the Mets pitching ace Tom Seaver gave up a home run to the first batter in the first game and the Mets lost 4-1, nobody expected the Mets to bounce back. But they did. With spectacular fielding, clutch hitting, and great pitching, the Mets swept the next four games and won the Series. This earned them the nickname "the Amazin' Mets."

1977—REGGIE! REGGIE! REGGIE!

In the 1977 World Series, the Yankees played the Dodgers. After five games, the Yankees led 3 games to 2. With one more victory they would be the World Champs. So the Yankees looked to their star of stars, slugger Reggie Jackson, to lead them. Could the man called "Mr. October" bring a World Series title to New York?

You bet! With 55,000 fans cheering in Yankee Stadium and millions more watching on TV, Reggie delivered. Three times he stepped up to the plate against three different Dodger pitchers. Each time he swung at the first pitch. And each time he sent the ball over the wall for a home run. Three pitches, three home runs—and another World Series championship for the Yankees. No one has ever equaled Reggie's World Series performance. And probably no one will.

1989: THE EARTHQUAKE SERIES

The 1989 World Series was sure to be a classic. The San Francisco Giants were playing the Oakland A's in the "Battle of the Bay Area." This Series would be the first time these two local teams had ever faced each other. After the first two games, which had been won easily by the A's at their home ballpark in Oakland, the Giants needed to shake things up, or the Series was going to be over in a hurry.

On October 17th, 60,000 fans packed into San Francisco's Candlestick Park. TV announcers were giving pre-game analysis, players were about to be introduced, and Giants

Left: Reggie Jackson during his Yankee days Right: Reggie at bat

fans were hoping for a win that might get their team back on track. Then nature entered the picture. A very strong earthquake, measuring 7.1 on the Richter scale, hit the San Francisco area. The stadium shook. Electrical power went out. The World Series stopped.

Luckily for fans at the game, the stadium received relatively little damage. Most people at the ballpark remained calm and only a few injuries were reported. When Baseball Commissioner Fay Vincent heard that power couldn't be restored quickly, he postponed the game. Fans left peacefully. Unfortunately, the rest of the San Francisco area hadn't made out so well. Highways and bridges collapsed, buildings fell, and fires raged. 67 people died. While the city coped with this disaster, Vincent postponed the World Series. He said that it was much less important than helping the people of San Francisco rebuild their city.

As things slowly returned to normal, some people felt that the World Series should continue as a way for the residents of the San Francisco area to focus on a happy event. Vincent agreed. Ten days after the earthquake, the A's beat the Giants in game 3. Then they won game 4 to win the series in a 4-0 sweep.

1993: THE TORONTO BLUE JAYS VS. THE PHILADELPHIA PHILLIES

"Every kid's dream." That's how Joe Carter described it. Carter's team, the Toronto Blue Jays, was playing the Philadelphia Phillies in the sixth game of the 1993 World Series. The Blue Jays led 3 games to 2, but the Phillies had just gone ahead in this game. If the Phillies won, the Series would be tied and the Phillies might have the momentum and confidence to win game seven.

It was the bottom of the ninth. The Blue Jays were down, 6 to 5. The Phillies had Mitch "Wild Thing" Williams on the mound. Williams was a hard-throwing but erratic (or wild) pitcher. He had given up a walk and a single. With one out and

runners on first and third, Carter came to the plate. The
count was two balls and two strikes when Williams delivered
a fastball. Carter swung and sent the ball soaring 379 feet
over the left field fence for the most famous home run in
World Series history. No one had ever hit a home run with his
team *trailing* in the game in the bottom of the ninth to win a
World Series. (Remember, Bill Mazeroski hit a game and Series
winner in 1960. But in that game, the Pirates and Yankees had
been tied.) And now Carter had done it. He accomplished
every boy's dream: to win a World Series with a home run!

DON LARSEN'S PERFECT GAME
IN THE 1956 WORLD SERIES

In 1956, the Yankees were once again facing the Brooklyn Dodgers in the World Series. It was the sixth time in ten years that these two teams would play for a Series title. Everyone expected a great matchup. After all, the Dodgers had Jackie Robinson and Duke Snider, and the Yankees had Whitey Ford, Mickey Mantle, and Yogi Berra. But no one expected heroics from Don Larsen, the Yankee pitcher who was about to make World Series history.

Each team had won two games. Larsen was scheduled to pitch for the Yankees in game five. He hadn't pitched very well in game two, which was won by the Dodgers. But in this game he pitched great. Dodger after Dodger stepped up to the plate, and Dodger after Dodger went back to the dugout without a hit.

Larsen was pitching a no-hitter in the World Series. No one had ever done that before. As the game went into the later innings, Larsen still had his no-hitter. In fact, Larsen was pitching a perfect game. No hits, no errors, and no walks.

In the ninth inning, the tension was mounting. The Yankees led 2-0. But the Dodgers would have three more outs to go. Larsen got two outs. Pinch hitter Dale Mitchell stepped to the plate. The first pitch Larsen threw was a ball. Larsen then got two strikes on Mitchell. The count was 1-2. One more strike, and Larsen would make baseball history. Larsen made his delivery. Mitchell held his swing, but the umpire called it a strike—strike three. Mitchell was out and Larsen was a baseball hero: the only pitcher ever to throw a perfect game in World Series history.

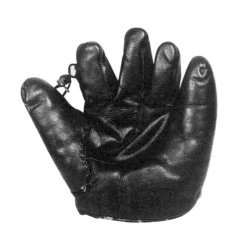

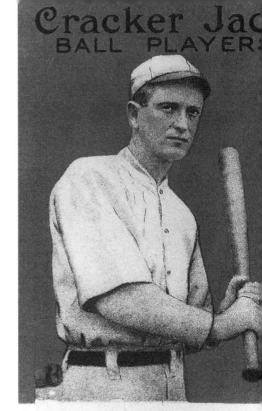

OAKES, PITTSBURGH - FEDERAL

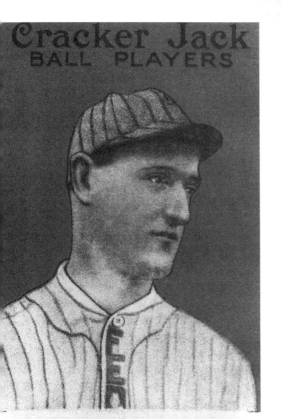

KAISERLING, INDIANAPOLIS - FEDERALS

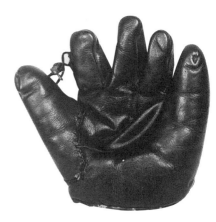

CHAPTER
5

Baseball Memorabilia

THE HALL OF FAME

Located in Cooperstown, New York, the Baseball Hall of Fame is a museum. First opened in 1939, the Hall of Fame includes exhibits on the history of baseball and displays about the great players of the game. Cooperstown was chosen because it was supposedly the place where Abner Doubleday invented the game. At the Hall of Fame, there are displays of uniforms, bats, and gloves of all the great players, from Babe Ruth and Ty Cobb to Hank Aaron and Nolan Ryan (for some strange reason, the Hall even has one of Babe Ruth's *bowling* balls). There are also exhibits paying tribute to the great Negro League players and the Women's League.

One of the best reasons to visit the Hall is to see how the sport has changed over the years. The Hall exhibits things from the past, like baseball gloves with no fingers, and more recent innovations in the game, like a piece of Astroturf™. But probably the best reason to go is to visit the actual Hall of Fame, the room where plaques of each of the elected members are on display. These plaques show a likeness of each player and list highlights of that player's accomplishments.

The Hall of Fame's main attraction is its yearly ceremony to honor the "new" inductees. Each year, eligible ex-players are voted upon by the Baseball Writers of America. A player must have played at least ten years in the majors and be retired from the game for five years before he can be elected to the Hall. Players who receive votes from at least 75% of the voters are elected. During the weekend of ceremonies and festivities, previous Hall inductees salute the new members. A baseball game, called the Hall of Fame Game, is played between two major league teams. Baseball fans from around the country pack Cooperstown to enjoy these star-studded events.

Besides honoring players, the Hall of Fame also acknowledges the contributions that other people have made to the game of baseball. Managers, umpires, sportswriters, broadcasters, executives, and pioneers of the game have also been elected to the Hall of Fame.

The first players were actually selected in 1936, a few years before the museum was ready to open. That year, five great players were selected—Ty Cobb, Babe Ruth, Honus Wagner, Christy Mathewson, and Walter Johnson.

One of the most famous speeches by a player being inducted into the Hall of Fame was given by Boston Red Sox superstar Ted Williams in 1966:

"I've been a very lucky guy to have worn a baseball uniform, to have struck out or to hit a tape-measure home run. And I hope someday the names of Satchel Paige and Josh Gibson in some way can be added as a symbol of the great Negro players who are not here only because they were not given a chance."

Five years later, in 1971, the Hall of Fame did honor the black players whom the majors had forgotten. In that year, a special Negro Leagues Committee began to select players from those leagues for inclusion in the Hall. A new wing in the Hall of Fame, dedicated to the great Negro Leagues players, was opened, and players like Josh Gibson and Cool Papa Bell were finally recognized.

In 1993, only one player was inducted—Reggie Jackson. Jackson, who played most of his career for the Oakland A's and New York Yankees, is best remembered for his long "tape-measure" home runs and clutch World Series play. Between the A's and Yankees, Jackson played on five World Series Championship teams. In his induction speech, Jackson graciously thanked the fans who supported him and the game.

1994 also saw only one player inducted. Steve Carlton, known as "Lefty," was a star pitcher for the St. Louis Cardinals and the Philadelphia Phillies. In January 1994, Hall of Fame voters elected Carlton in the first year of his eligibility. Carlton was a four-time Cy Young Award winner and was second only to Nolan Ryan in career strikeouts.

In addition to Carlton, two famous old-timers, Phil Rizzuto and Leo Durocher, were selected by the Hall of Fame Veterans Committee. Nicknamed "The Scooter," Rizzuto was a shortstop for the New York Yankees. In his thirteen-year playing career, Rizzuto was a five-time All-Star and the American League's MVP in 1950. He played on eight Yankee World Championship teams. A long-time television broadcaster with the Yankees, the Scooter has remained a popular figure in baseball.

Leo "the Lip" Durocher managed in the majors for twenty-six years. During that time, he posted 2,008 wins with four teams. Nicknamed "the Lip" for the way he argued with umpires, Durocher won three pennants (including the famous Bobby Thompson homer game) and a World Series. Durocher will be honored posthumously. He died in 1991, after having lived to the age of 86.

BASEBALL CARD & MEMORABILIA COLLECTING

Today, baseball cards are everywhere. The sports card industry is a billion-dollar business. Kids and collectors alike visit thousands of card shows each year where they buy, sell, and trade all sorts of memorabilia—from cards and auto-graphed bats and balls to players' jerseys and caps. But how did the baseball card industry get started?

Some of the earliest baseball cards were produced in 1887. Tobacco companies included them in packages of ciga-rettes. The cards made at that time were smaller and looked very different from today's colorful, glossy cards.

Probably the most famous of the tobacco company card sets were those printed by the American Tobacco Company. Between 1909 and 1911, this company produced a set of 524 cards, known to collectors as the T206 set. This set included one of the rarest, and the most expensive, baseball cards ever produced—the Honus Wagner card (*see the sidebar*).

In the 1930s, there came a change in card manufacturing that most kids—and some dentists—remember well. At this time most cards began to be packaged with bubble gum. The two main card producers of this era were the Goudey Gum

Company and Gum, Inc., which later became the Bowman Gum Company. Bowman's 1948 set of 48 cards is said to be the first set of the modern era of card collecting. Bowman, along with a new company called Topps, became the main card producers from 1951 to 1955. Topps's 1952 set includes another of the most sought-after cards—the Mickey Mantle rookie card. From '51 to '55, Topps and Bowman competed. They signed baseball players to exclusive contracts which forbade them from being portrayed on cards made by other companies. This is why these sets didn't have complete rosters of every major league team.

In 1956, Topps bought the Bowman Company. From 1956 to 1980, Topps controlled the card market. They signed just about every major league player to an exclusive contract. From 1952 to 1973, Topps distributed its cards in series. That is, they sent out only a portion of the complete set during each part of the year. The cards from the later series—which were usually distributed toward the end of the baseball season—were often harder to find. This made these cards rarer, and thus worth more to collectors. Topps stopped this practice in 1974.

1981 was another key year for the card-collecting hobby. That year, another company, the Fleer Corporation, successfully sued to be able to print baseball cards, as well. This opened up the card market to many companies.

While most of today's cards are produced in large quantities that keep scarcity and investment prices down, card companies also produce limited-run premium card sets. These cards are sold in smaller quantities and at higher prices.

TIPS FOR COLLECTING CARDS

Baseball cards can be worth a lot of money. Some cards of famous old players can cost thousands of dollars today. More recent cards can also fetch a nice price—Rickey Henderson's 1980 Topps rookie card, for example, can fetch a price of $200—but only if it is in mint condition.

Collectors purchase cards for different reasons. Younger fans will buy packs of cards and trade cards with friends. Other fans like to get cards of their favorite players or team. Some collectors try to get complete sets of cards made by particular companies. Still others collect cards as an investment, since baseball cards often go up in price each year. As the hobby has grown, and more and more people are vying for the rarer cards, prices have skyrocketed.

Here are a few things to keep in mind when collecting and buying baseball cards as an investment:

(1) *Check the card's quality*. The best cards are MINT CONDITION cards. These are cards that are not damaged in any way. Prices will drop considerably for cards with any

mint   fair   poor

wear—creased, rounded edges or tears. Price guides (books which list the general cost of specific cards) will list prices for cards in a range of conditions: from MINT to EXCELLENT, VERY GOOD, GOOD, FAIR, and POOR.

(2) *Rookie cards.* One way to get potentially valuable cards at low prices is to buy rookie cards. These are the first cards printed for a particular player or set of players. The rookie card of a player who later becomes famous is usually valuable because few people bothered to keep the card (because nobody knew he would be a star). In the past, card companies didn't print very many rookie cards, adding to their scarcity and price. Today, however, many people know to collect rookie cards, and companies print lots and lots of cards, so prices have not been as high as they have in the past. Here's a sample of what some superstar rookie cards are worth to collectors:

> Mickey Mantle—1952 Topps rookie card $23,000
> Nolan Ryan—1968 Topps rookie card $1400

Pete Rose—1963 Topps rookie card, $600

Rickey Henderson—1980 Topps rookie card, $200

(3) *Star cards*. Collecting any cards of famous players is also wise, though not as lucrative as rookie cards because companies usually print a large number of these players' cards. Star cards, though, will always be worth a little (and sometimes, a lot) more than average player— or common—cards.

THE HONUS WAGNER CARD

The Honus Wagner card of 1910 recently sold for $451,000! It's so expensive because it is very rare. In the early years of card collecting, tobacco companies sold cards along with their cigarettes and cigars. Wagner, a star with the Pittsburgh Pirates, supposedly didn't want his name associated with a tobacco company because he didn't want those people who collected cards to become addicted to cigarettes. Wagner made the American Tobacco Company destroy the cards with his likeness on them. But not all the cards were destroyed. A few had been distributed before Wagner complained.

(4) *Rare and mistake cards.* Scarcity affects card prices greatly. Some cards are rare because they were mistakes. Often, a company will catch an error in printing (like putting the wrong player's picture on a card) and issue a corrected card. The few mistake cards that are sold go up in price because of their relative scarcity.

(5) *Protect your valuables.* Because the value of your collection is related to the condition of your cards, you should keep them in a safe place. Cards should be protected from water and humidity, and from any other physical damage. Hobby stores sell cardboard boxes (for complete sets), and albums (for smaller sets and individual cards) with plastic binders that hold cards. You can also buy individual holders for your rarer cards.

(6) *Look for antique cards.* Of course, the luckiest way to start a card collection is to check your parents' or grandparents' attic or closet for the shoebox that might make you a pile of money. You never know—maybe Dad was a collector and forgot about those Mickey Mantles and Ty Cobbs he socked away.

The Best: Yesterday, Today and Tomorrow

Some of the most fun baseball fans have is deciding who the greatest players of all-time are and were. Fans used to argue over whether Willie Mays or Mickey Mantle or Duke Snider was the best centerfielder. People wonder whether Nolan Ryan could have struck out Babe Ruth, or whether Ted Williams could have hit .400 against flame-throwers like Dwight Gooden. Today, fans debate whether Ken Griffey, Jr. or Barry Bonds is the Major League's best. One way to prove who was or is the best, is to look at the statistics players compiled during their careers. These stats help us rate the game's greatest. Take a look at these career and single-season stat leaders. Then read further about some past and future stars:

Career Leaders

Career Home Run Leaders

Hank Aaron	755
Babe Ruth	714
Willie Mays	660
Frank Robinson	568
Harmon Killebrew	573
Reggie Jackson	563
Mike Schmidt	548
Mickey Mantle	536
Jimmie Foxx	534
Ted Williams	521
Willie McCovey	521

3,000 Hit Club

Pete Rose	4256
Ty Cobb	4191
Hank Aaron	3771
Stan Musial	3630
Tris Speaker	3515
Carl Yastrzemski	3419
Honus Wagner	3418
Eddie Collins	3311
Willie Mays	3283
Nap Lajoie	3244
George Brett	3154
Paul Waner	3152
Robin Yount	3142
Rod Carew	3053
Lou Brock	3023
Dave Winfield	3014
Al Kaline	3007

Roberto Clemente	3000
Cap Anson	3000

Career Batting Average

Ty Cobb	.367
Rogers Hornsby	.358
Joe Jackson	.356
Ed Delahanty	.346
Tris Speaker	.345
Ted Williams	.344
Billy Hamilton	.344
Willie Keeler	.343
Dan Brouthers	.342
Babe Ruth	.342
Harry Heilmann	.342

Career Wins

Cy Young	511
Walter Johnson	416
Christy Mathewson	373
Grover Alexander	373
Warren Spahn	363
Kid Nichols	361
Pud Galvin	361
Tim Keefe	342
Steve Carlton	329
Eddie Plank	327

Career Saves

Lee Smith	401
Jeff Reardon	365
Rollie Fingers	341
Goose Gossage	309
Bruce Sutter	300

Dennis Eckersley	275
Tom Henke	260
Dave Righetti	252
Dan Quisenberry	244
Sparky Lyle	238

Career Strikeouts

Nolan Ryan	5714
Steve Carlton	4136
Bert Blyleven	3701
Tom Seaver	3640
Don Sutton	3574
Gaylord Perry	3534
Walter Johnson	3508
Phil Niekro	3342
Ferguson Jenkins	3192
Bob Gibson	3117

Single Season Records (since 1900)

Hits

George Sisler (1920)	257

Runs Batted In

Hack Wilson (1930)	190

Home Runs

Roger Maris (1961)	61

Batting Average

Hugh Duffy (1894)	.438

Stolen Bases

Rickey Henderson (1982)	130

Wins
Jack Chesbro (1904)   41

Saves
Bobby Thigpen (1990)   57

Strikeouts
Nolan Ryan (1973)   383

Triple Crown Winners
(league leader in HRs, RBIs, and BA in the same season)

National League		HR	RBI	BA
Paul Hines	1878	4	50	.358
Hugh Duffy	1894	18	145	.438
Heinie Zimmerman	1912	14	103	.372
Rogers Hornsby	1922	42	152	.401
	1925	39	143	.403
Chuck Klein	1933	28	120	.368
Joe Medwick	1937	31	154	.374

American League				
Nap Lajoie	1901	14	125	.422
Ty Cobb	1909	9	107	.377
Jimmie Foxx	1933	48	163	.356
Lou Gehrig	1934	9	165	.363
Ted Williams	1942	36	137	.356
	1947	32	114	.343
Mickey Mantle	1956	52	130	.353
Frank Robinson	1966	49	122	.316
Carl Yastrzemski	1967	44	121	.326

Single Game Records (9-inning games, since 1900)

Most Hits

Rennie Stennett (Sept 16, 1975)	7

Most Home Runs

Lou Gehrig (June 3, 1932)	4

Gil Hodges (Aug 31, 1950)

Joe Adcock (July 31, 1954)

Rocky Colavito (June 10, 1959)

Willie Mays (April 30, 1961)

Bob Horner (July 6, 1986)

Mark Whiten (Sept 7, 1993)

Most RBIs

	12

Jim Bottomley (Sept 16, 1924)

Mark Whiten (Sept 7, 1993)

Most Strikeouts

Roger Clemens (April 29, 1986)	20

OTHER PAST STARS:

Henry Aaron "Hammerin' Hank" was the nickname of this Hall of Fame slugger. Aaron, who played in the majors from 1955 to 1976, hit a Major League record 755 home runs.

Aaron played most of his career for the Braves (a team which played in Milwaukee and then moved to Atlanta). At the end of his career, Aaron returned to Milwaukee, where he was a designated hitter for the Brewers.

Ted Williams Nicknamed "The Splendid Splinter," Williams was one of baseball's top hitters. Playing for the Boston Red Sox, Williams won two American League Most Valuable Player awards. His lifetime batting average of .344 ranks among the game's best. Williams was the last person to bat over .400 for a single season. He did this in 1941, when he batted .406.

Roberto Clemente The Puerto Rican-born Clemente was a superstar outfielder for the Pittsburgh Pirates. He totaled an amazing 3,000 hits in a career that lasted from 1955 to 1972. Clemente won the National League MVP Award in 1966 and helped lead the Pirates to two World Series championships. Clemente's career was tragically cut short. He died in a plane crash while on his way to deliver supplies to earthquake victims in Nicaragua. Waiving the usual five-year-retirement clause, the Baseball Hall of Fame elected Clemente posthumously into the Hall in 1973.

Ty Cobb Known as the "Georgia Peach," Cobb was one of the best hitters of all time. He holds the record for the highest career batting average and was one of the first players elected to the Hall of Fame. An outfielder, Cobb played from 1905 to 1928. He played most of his career with the Detroit Tigers, though he played his last two seasons for the Philadelphia Athletics. Cobb was an intense competitor. In fact, he was hated by many opposing players, and not just for his terrific talent. Cobb was known to have sharpened the metal spikes on his baseball shoes to injure fielders as they tried to tag him out on the bases.

TODAY'S STARS—AND TOMORROW'S

Cecil Fielder Many people compare this Detroit Tiger slugger with another large home-run king, Babe Ruth. The first baseman Fielder is a big man and he hits homers like Ruth. Fielder knocks in a lot of runs as well. He led the American League in RBIs for three consecutive seasons (1990-92).

Ken Griffey, Jr. Baseball experts say Griffey, Jr. does it all. He hits for a high batting average, he hits home runs (in 1993, he slammed 45 four-baggers), he steals bases, and he catches everything hit to him in the outfield. Griffey got his baseball genes from his father, Ken Griffey, Sr., who played many years in the majors as well. A now, perennial All-Star, Griffey, Jr. is leading the Seattle Mariners on the road to respectability.

Barry Bonds Bonds is perhaps the most famous of this "new breed." He is a great player who combines speed and power. In 1993, Bonds came close to winning the Triple Crown. He led the National League in homers (with 46) and RBIs (with 123). His .336 batting average was not quite enough to win the batting title. Still, Bonds is acknowledged as one of the game's best. He is also the highest-paid player in the game. After the 1992 season, Bonds became a free agent. The Pittsburgh Pirates could not afford to sign him, so he went to the San Francisco Giants, who had offered him an amazing $43-million-dollar contract. Fans of the game wondered if anyone was really worth that amount of money. Well, right from the start of the season, Bonds proved he was worth it.

Like Ken Griffey, Jr., Bonds is the son of an ex-major league player. Bonds' father, Bobby, who had a long and distinguished playing career, is now a coach with the Giants.

Juan Gonzalez Another one of the American League's rising stars is the Texas Rangers' Juan Gonzalez. Gonzalez finished the 1993 season leading the American League in homers (with 46). He also knocked in 118 RBIs for the Rangers.

Jack McDowell This White Sox star is one of the game's top young pitchers. In 1993, McDowell led the American League in victories with 22. Helping the White Sox win the American League West Division title, McDowell was named the American League Cy Young Award winner, given each year to the best pitcher in the league.

Frank Thomas Playing first base for the Chicago White Sox, Thomas is known as "The Big Hurt" for the big hurt he puts on baseballs as he sends them flying out of the park. Thomas' stats for 1993 ranked him as a leader in all the power categories. He hit 41 home runs and had 128 RBIs.

Ace: A team's top starting pitcher.

Assist: A throw made by one player that helps another player make a putout. For example, when a shortstop fields a ground ball and throws it to first base, he gets an assist and the first baseman records a putout.

Balk: An illegal motion made by the pitcher before he throws a pitch; often meant to deceive a base runner.

"Boot": Slang term for an error.

"Cleanup" Hitter: Name given to the fourth batter in the starting lineup. This player is usually a home-run hitter with power to drive in, or "clean" the bases of, runners.

The "Cycle": The name given to hitting a single, double, triple, and home run in one game.

Cy Young Award: Named after Cy Young, the pitcher who won a record 511 games in his career, this award is given to the best pitcher in each league.

Designated Hitter (DH): A player who bats for another player, usually the pitcher, but does not field his position. Used in the American, but not the National League.

Earned Run Average (ERA): The average number of earned runs given up by a pitcher for every nine innings.

Free Agent: name given to a player whose contract expires. When this happens, he is free to sign a new contract with any team.

Gopher Ball: Nickname for a pitch which is hit for a home run.

Hot Corner: A nickname for the third base position because the third baseman often has to play close to the batter and must field a lot of hard-hit shots.

No-Hitter: A game in which a pitcher does not allow the opposing teams any hits.

Official Scorer: A person watching the game, usually a local sportswriter, who decides whether certain plays are hits or errors, wild pitches, or passed balls.

Passed Ball: A pitch that the catcher should catch but which he misses, thus allowing a runner to advance to another base.

Perfect Game: A no-hitter in which no batters from the other team even reach first base.

Pinch-Hitter: A player who is sent up to bat for another player.

Run Batted In (RBI): A run that scores as a result of a hit, a walk, or sacrifice fly by a batter.

Relief Pitcher: A pitcher who comes in for another pitcher. Another name for a relief pitcher is "fireman."

Round-Tripper: Slang term for a home-run; so named because the batter gets a trip around all the bases.

Sacrifice Fly: A fly ball caught for an out after which a base runner tags up and scores. The player who hit the ball receives an RBI.

Save: Earned by a reliever who comes in and preserves a lead for his team.

Southpaw: A left-handed pitcher.

Switch-Hitter: A player who can bat left-handed as well as right-handed.

Triple Crown: When a single player leads his league in a single season in batting average, home runs, and runs batted in.

Wild Pitch: A throw from the pitcher which the catcher cannot be expected to have caught and which allows a runner to advance to another base.

BIBLIOGRAPHY

Beckett, James. *The Sport Americana Baseball Card Price Guide.*

Browne, Lois. *Girls of Summer: In Their Own League.*

Kirk, Troy. *Collector's Guide to Baseball Cards.* Radnor, Pennsylvania: Wallace-Homestead Book Company, 1990.

Regosin, Donn. *Invisible Men: Life in Baseball's Negro Leagues.* New York: Atheneum, 1983.

Reichler, Joseph. *The Baseball Encyclopedia.* New York: Macmillan Publishing Co., 1993.

Seymour, Harold. *Baseball: The Early Years.* New York: Oxford University Press, 1960.